"We delight in the beauty of the butterfly, but rarely admit the changes it has gone through to achieve that beauty."

Maya Angelou

butterfly speaks

by nora oz

iiPUBLISHING

butterfly speaks

Copyright © 2021 by nora oz

Cover design by tonii

ISBN: 979-8-9850204-1-0

Printed in the United States of America

ii PUBLISHING

foreword

A butterfly is merely a flying catepillar.
We are evolved versions of what we once were.
And although we change, we (all versions of self) still remain.

The past lives in the present and both transition into the future.
So appreciate every stage of growth and change,
Knowing the egg, the larva, and the chrysallis
All speak in the whisper of the butterfly's wings.

Enjoy the metamorphosis in these pages.

-tonii

contents

egg - 1

larva - 29

chrysalis - 57

winged - 83

ROWTH. LIFE BEGINS. FERTILITY. BEGINNING. COMFORT ZONE. NEW. BABY
ATCHING. LIFE. GROWTH. LIFE BEGINS. FERTILITY. BEGINNING. C
TRENGTH. MAYBE. EMBRYO. HATCHING. LIFE. SMALL. GROWTH. LIFE BEG
IRTH. CROWN. CURIOSITY. STRENGTH. MAYBE. EMBRYO. HATCHING. LIFE
OTENTIAL. FRAGILE. CARE. BIRTH. CROWN. CURIOSITY. STRENGTH. MAY
OMFORT ZONE. NEW. BABY. POTENTIAL. FRAGILE. CARE. BIRTH. CROWN
EGINS. FERTILITY. BEGINNING. COMFORT ZONE. NEW. BABY. POTENTIAL.
IFE. SMALL. GROWTH. LIFE BEGINS. FERTILITY. BEGINNING. COMFORT Z
AYBE. EMBRYO. HATCHING. LIFE. SMALL. GROWTH. LIFE BEGINS. FERTILIT
URIOSITY. STRENGTH. MAYBE. EMBRYO. HATCHING. LIFE. SMALL. GRO
RAGILE. CARE. BIRTH. CROWN. CURIOSITY. STRENGTH. MAYBE. EMBRYO
ONE. NEW. BABY. POTENTIAL. FRAGILE. CARE. BIRTH. CROWN. CURIOS
ERTILITY. BEGINNING. COMFORT ZONE. NEW. BABY. POTENTIAL. FRAGI
MALL. GROWTH. LIFE BEGINS. FERTILITY. BEGINNING. COMFORT ZONE. N
MBRYO. HATCHING. LIFE. SMALL. GROWTH. LIFE BEGINS. FERTILITY. B
URIOSITY. STRENGTH. MAYBE. EMBRYO. HATCHING. LIFE. SMALL. GRO
RAGILE. CARE. BIRTH. CROWN. CURIOSITY. STRENGTH. MAYBE. EMBRY
ONE. NEW. BABY. POTENTIAL. FRAGILE. CARE. BIRTH. CROWN. CURIOS
ERTILITY. BEGINNING. COMFORT ZONE. NEW. BABY. POTENTI GI
MALL. GROWTH. LIFE BEGINS. FERTILITY. BEGINNING. COMFORT ZONE. N
MBRYO. HATCHING. LIFE. SMALL. GROWTH. LIFE BEGINS. F
URIOSITY. STRENGTH. MAYBE. EMBRYO. HATCHI
RAGILE. CARE. BIRTH. CROWN. CU
ONE. NEW. BABY. POTENTIAL. FRAGILE. CARE. BIRTH. CROWN.
ERTILITY. BEGINNING. COMFORT ZONE. NEW. BABY. POTENTIA
MALL. GROWTH. LIFE BEGINS. FERTILITY. BEGINNING. COMFORT
MBRYO. HATCHING. LIFE. SMALL. GROWTH. LIFE BEGINS. FERTILITY
URIOSITY. STRENGTH. MAYBE. EMBRYO. HATCHING. LIFE. SMALL. G
RAGILE. CARE. BIRTH. CROWN. CURIOSITY. STRENGTH. MAYBE. EME
ONE. NEW. BABY. POTENTIAL. FRAGILE. CARE. BIRTH. CROWN. C
ERTILITY. BEGINNING. COMFORT ZONE. NEW. BABY. POTENTIAL. FRAG
MALL. GROWTH. LIFE BEGINS. FERTILITY. BEGINNING. COMFORT ZONE.
MBRYO. HATCHING. LIFE. SMALL. GROWTH. LIFE BEGINS. FERTILITY.
URIOSITY. STRENGTH. MAYBE. EMBRYO. HATCHING. LIFE. SMALL. GR
RAGILE. CARE. BIRTH. CROWN. CURIOSITY. STRENGTH. MAYBE. EMBRYO
EW. BABY. POTENTIAL. FRAGILE. CARE. BIRTH. CROWN. CURIOSITY. ST
EGINNING. COMFORT ZONE. NEW. BABY. POTENTIAL. FRAGILE. CARE
ROWTH. LIFE BEGINS. FERTILITY. BEGINNING. COMFORT ZONE. NEW. BAE
ATCHING. LIFE. SMALL. GROWTH. LIFE BEGINS. FERTILITY. BEGINNINC
TRENGTH. MAYBE. EMBRYO. HATCHING. LIFE. SMALL. GROWTH. LIFE B
IRTH. CROWN. CURIOSITY. STRENGTH. MAYBE. EMBRYO. HATCHING. LI
OTENTIAL. FRAGILE. CARE. BIRTH. CROWN. CURIOSITY. STRENGTH. M
OMFORT ZONE. NEW. BABY. POTENTIAL. FRAGILE. CARE. BIRTH. CRO
EGINS. FERTILITY. BEGINNING. COMFORT ZONE. NEW. BABY. POTENTIA
FE. SMALL. GROWTH. LIFE BEGINS. FERTILITY. BEGINNING. COMFORT

L. FRAGILE. CARE. BIRTH. CROWN. CURIOSITY. STRENGTH. MAYBE. EMBRY(
ONE. NEW. BABY. POTENTIAL. FRAGILE. CARE. BIRTH. CROWN. CURIOSIT
ITY. BEGINNING. COMFORT ZONE. NEW. BABY. POTENTIAL. FRAGILE. CAR
ROWTH. LIFE BEGINS. FERTILITY. BEGINNING. COMFORT ZONE. NEW. BAB
O. HATCHING. LIFE. SMALL. GROWTH. LIFE BEGINS. FERTILITY. BEGINNIN(
Y. STRENGTH. MAYBE. EMBRYO. HATCHING. LIFE. SMALL. GROWTH. LIF
ARE. BIRTH. CROWN. CURIOSITY. STRENGTH. MAYBE. EMBRYO. HATCHIN(
ABY. POTENTIAL. FRAGILE. CARE. BIRTH. CROWN. CURIOSITY. STRENGT
G. COMFORT ZONE. NEW. BABY. POTENTIAL. FRAGILE. CARE. BIRTH. CROW
EGINS. FERTILITY. BEGINNING. COMFORT ZONE. NEW. BABY. POTENTIA
G. LIFE. SMALL. GROWTH. LIFE BEGINS. FERTILITY. BEGINNING. COMFOI
GTH. MAYBE. EMBRYO. HATCHING. LIFE. SMALL. GROWTH. LIFE BEGIN
RTH. CROWN. CURIOSITY. STRENGTH. MAYBE. EMBRYO. HATCHING. LIF
OTENTIAL. FRAGILE. CARE. BIRTH. CROWN. CURIOSITY. STRENGTH. MAYB
OMFORT ZONE. NEW. BABY. POTENTIAL. FRAGILE. CARE. BIRTH. CROW
EGINS. FERTILITY. BEGINNING. COMFORT ZONE. NEW. BABY. POTENTIA
. LIFE. SMALL. GROWTH. LIFE BEGINS. FERTILITY. BEGINNING. COMFOI
TH. MAYBE. EMBRYO. HATCHING. LIFE. SMALL. GROWTH. LIFE BEGIN
RTH. CROWN. CURIOSITY. STRENGTH. MAYBE. EMBRYO. HATCHING. LIF
TENTIAL. FRAGILE. CARE. BIRTH. CROWN. CURIOSITY. STRENGTH. MAYB
OMFORT ZONE. NEW. BABY. POTENTIAL. FRAGILE. CARE. BIRTH. CROW
NS. FERTILITY. BEGINNING. **EGG** COMFORT ZONE. NEW. BABY. POTENTIA
. LIFE. SMALL. GROWTH. LIFE BEGINS. FERTILITY. BEGINNING. COMFOI
TH. MAYBE. EMBRYO. HATCHING. LIFE. SMALL. GROWTH. LIFE BEGIN
RTH. CROWN. CURIOSITY. STRENGTH. MAYBE. EMBRYO. HATCHING. LIF
TENTIAL. FRAGILE. CARE. BIRTH. CROWN. CURIOSITY. STRENGTH. MAYB
OMFORT ZONE. NEW. BABY. POTENTIAL. FRAGILE. CARE. BIRTH. CROW
GINS. FERTILITY. BEGINNING. COMFORT ZONE. NEW. BABY. POTENTIA
LIFE. SMALL. GROWTH. LIFE BEGINS. FERTILITY. BEGINNING. COMFOI
TH. MAYBE. EMBRYO. HATCHING. LIFE. SMALL. GROWTH. LIFE BEGIN
TH. CROWN. CURIOSITY. STRENGTH. MAYBE. EMBRYO. HATCHING. LIF
TENTIAL. FRAGILE. CARE. BIRTH. CROWN. CURIOSITY. STRENGTH. MAYB
MFORT ZONE. NEW. BABY. POTENTIAL. FRAGILE. CARE. BIRTH. CROW
GINS. FERTILITY. BEGINNING. COMFORT ZONE. NEW. BABY. POTENTIA
E. SMALL. GROWTH. LIFE BEGINS. FERTILITY. BEGINNING. COMFORT ZON
E. EMBRYO. HATCHING. LIFE. SMALL. GROWTH. LIFE BEGINS. FERTILIT
N. CURIOSITY. STRENGTH. MAYBE. EMBRYO. HATCHING. LIFE. SMAL
FRAGILE. CARE. BIRTH. CROWN. CURIOSITY. STRENGTH. MAYBE. EMBRY
E. NEW. BABY. POTENTIAL. FRAGILE. CARE. BIRTH. CROWN. CURIOSIT
Y. BEGINNING. COMFORT ZONE. NEW. BABY. POTENTIAL. FRAGILE. CAR
WTH. LIFE BEGINS. FERTILITY. BEGINNING. COMFORT ZONE. NEW. BAB
HATCHING. LIFE. SMALL. GROWTH. LIFE BEGINS. FERTILITY. BEGINNIN
STRENGTH. MAYBE. EMBRYO. HATCHING. LIFE. SMALL. GROWTH. LI
E. BIRTH. CROWN. CURIOSITY. STRENGTH. MAYBE. EMBRYO. HATCHIN
BY. POTENTIAL. FRAGILE. CARE. BIRTH. CROWN. CURIOSITY. STRENGT

memory

A brown arm extends,
    reaches
    working against the orange stroke of a
    motion passed.
Dance is not meant to be frozen.
    the colors enhance
    the bend of the knee,
    the quick turn of a neck,
    But...
    dance was never meant to be
    sedentary.
Can she see the beads of sweat,
    born from the dancers attempt to be
    free?
Yes, she can!
They want to move...
They want to move...
She wants to move...
Staring on,
    as the colors from the everyday sunset
    play with those from the ever
    mysterious dance.

Eager faces seem to smile,
        as their movements change into the next step.
An orange stroke glides
        from left
        to right,
        leaving behind the swishing sound
        of beautiful silk garments.
A brown
        reaching arm
        finds its way, at a snail's pace,
        to the fingertips of its wanted
        destination.
Triumphant laughing can be heard
        as the purple of the sun
        mixes with a stroke of red
        the bended knee straightens…
A dance begins!
Smells of dry heat and incense invade the nostril.
Brown arms
        reaching
        for their partners,
        to continue with their joy:
        the dancing.

Feet pick up off the ground,
                    as the rust of the sunset mixes
                    with the yellow stroke of an
                    extended body.
Let it go on
                    please,
                    she begs,
                    but then the last ray of rust disappears
                    from the glass in the frame.
The light fades,
                    and the dance is unmoving,
                    unchanging
                    again
A brown arm
                    reaches,
                    once more,
                    as if it had never met its goal
                    as she had seen

Magic fades with the light.
Tears swell with the dark.
A final whisper of goodbye,
                as she flees from the warm place
                that was her home.
From the mysterious dance,
                from the beauty of the colors,
                the swish of the garments
                smells of a faraway place
                that could always be reached
                through that dance.
Her sedentary dance.
Her dance.

Her *home.*

home

The streets buzz with stories
　　　　　　of past lives and memories;
Beloved footsteps on concrete,
　　　　　　walked strongly
　　　　　　over deep rooted cracks;
Paint splattered cobblestones,
　　　　　　danced to Caribbean beats,
　　　　　　on eves of new school years.
Air permeated with spices
　　　　　　that traveled from restaurants,
　　　　　　and memories of factories.

It still looks like industry
　　　　　　should be making its mark here,
　　　　　　but all that is left is the feeling…
　　　　　　of *wanting*…

to be *better*.

faith

My grandmother has faith,
          that God will watch over her family,
          when she is gone.

Childhood memories of her cigarette smoke
          stained prayers
          over my head,
          and efforts to make church more enjoyable
          with cinnamon Dentyne gum,
          makes me believe her.
She gives me her faith.

My father has faith
          that despite what the doctors say,
          his overconsumption of food will not
          kill him.

Childhood memories of his heavy,
          sleeveless, blanket wide arms,
          covering me from head to toe,
          and his boisterous laugh
          over our 3rd slice of cake,
          makes me believe him.
He gives me his faith.

My mother has faith
          that as long as she stays true to herself,
          she will find a form of happiness
          in her unsatisfying life.
Childhood memories of her smiling face,
          entering our railroad apartment with dinner plans
          of pasta and… tomatoes?
          - because that is what the fridge provided,
          makes me believe her.
She gives me her faith.

I carry their faith,
> as the building blocks of my own.
> the foundation is as shaky as their
> sensibilities,
> but they are my home.

I have faith
> in the fact that I have no idea what I want;
> and that is ok.
> Because I have my mother's faith to guide my way.

I have faith
> in joyful indulgences
> and the pain that comes
> with destructive decisions.

Because I have my father's faith to teach me.

I have faith
> that God works in mysterious
> and fucked up ways!
> servants are taken away
> when their message was made,
> even if their granddaughter can't make it to the
> hospital bed.

Love lives on.

Because I have my grandmother's faith to warm me.

Faith is,
> by definition,
> the complete trust,
> or confidence,
> in someone or something.

I have *faith*…

interpersonal communication

Q: Have you ever thought about why you communicate?

No,

I haven't.
>   because communicating for me
>   is like breathing.

We survive by breathing.

I breathe by writing.

I write for communication.

And communicating, for me, is breathing
>   when my pen hits paper
>   a feeling arises within
>   similar to that of Beethoven
>   when his fingers hit keys
>   he could hear.
>   he could live.

I can breathe.
>   and of the 3 needs
>   that communication meets
>   the only one that applies to me
>   is control
>   because I want you all to know
>   that my presence on this paper
>   is not the first nor the last.

I am the woman slave,
                who became the first African-American
                to write a poem

I am the girl who asked why
                she could not write words to a
                pentameter

I am Emily Dickinson

I am Nikki Giovanni

I am Maya Angelou

I am a writer

I am a communicator
                and I can breathe.
                that's why I communicate,

I already knew that!
                no need to think about it.

summer lovin'

Summer in Brooklyn smells like fresh cut
        grass
        and heat dried piss;
        newly bloomed tree leaves
        and garbage.

A cool breeze helps one live through
        the humidity of city days
        as flip flops battle against adhesive tar streets.

Flies buzz around in the absence of
        mosquitoes.

Summer in Brooklyn sounds like
        the ring of tricycle bells
        and honking horns;
        as playground children
        hail the Spanish women
        for piraguas in urban parks.

It still fascinates me that I can be immersed in
        the rustle of trees,
        the chirping of crickets,
        tweets of birds,
        and the silence of a forest
        then turn a corner and be hit by the blare of
        traffic on Flatbush.

I sit in quiet outside seating,
        the enclave of my little pizzeria
        and forget for a moment that I am in
        Brooklyn.

I could be anywhere,
        and I am here.

Why would anyone leave New York
        to go to a new country,
        when every country comes here?

18

cap
gown
toss
laugh
cry
wave goodbye
sigh hello
hall
dorm
        getting to know
        how to live with strangers
nervous laughter
high fives
inside jokes
forever roomies
        getting to know
        freedom of my body
thighs
eyes
lips
tits
ass
hands
mine all mine
        getting to know
        freedom of my time

call crawl
sleep dance
talk drink
study
eat
contemplate
my fate
1st semester failed
        getting to know
        how to bounce back
Ne-Yo soothes
Drake inspires
Twerk out frustration
Whine my desires
I am eternity,
nestled in curves
of my decisions.
And the world
is holding its breath
to witness my next,
sensual step
acting on inspired ideals
to magnanimous moments.

I am what you've been waiting for!

sick

no runny nose.
no clammy hands.
no phlegm cough.
no phlegm.
        just brick cold body
        radiating August summer heat,
        shredded & scorched sore throat,
        preventing digestion,
        and NOW,
        finalizing fatigue.
Definitely can't move:
        weak arms abide by illness' reign…
Definitely can't speak!
        trapped air wheezing at illness'
        whim…
        just have to lie, and wait.
        wait for comforting sleep,
        wait for releasing death,
        wait for my matter of fact mother to call,
        with practical advice to see a doctor.

open to all options.

i want to be a billionaire so freaking bad

buy all of the things I never had.
I don't need fame
or everyone to know my name
I just want
        to spend my days
        without worrying
        if the next check will go my way
        cover my bills and my pills
        so I can live another day
I want to be a billionaire…
        so.
        freaking.
        bad.
ace all of my classes because I'm not worried
        about tuition
fulfill every dream because it would be the
        full life I'm living
I would swim and dance;
        drive and travel in a trance
        jumping from place to place,
        breathing in the air of foreign lands.
I want to be a billionaire so freaking bad!
        why is it that to succeed
        i have to work 40x harder
        but to fail
        it only takes 1 mistake?
can I get
        One
        break?
a little lotto ticket with my name all over it
        can give me the chance
        to fix things up
        and make it more stable

I want to be a billionaire so freaking bad
        buy all of the things I never had:
        a college degree
        a house for my mom and me
        a car
        adult dance classes
        guitar lessons
        plane tickets to where ever
        an iTouch
        every Gustav Klimt I've ever wanted
        all the clothes I admire
        custom made shoes
        tickets to the TCM film festival
        my bedroom, fully designed by myself,
        to be my true sanctuary
        time to volunteer
        time to fall in love
        a knowledge of the date,
        (because monotony no longer blends the
        days together)
        time to spend with friends
        time to talk with my sister
        peace of body.
        peace of mind.
        peace of spirit.

they say money can't buy you happiness….
        but it sure as hell makes things easier!
I want to be a billionaire
        so.
        freaking.
        bad…
buy all of the things *I've never had.*

lyrical poem

Just like a star across my sky
Inspirational & unattainable I
Whisper wishes to your presence
Impenetrable in its obliviousness
Of my pleading, drilling eyes
Centered on the silver stitching
            on the back
            of your *blue suede dinner jacket.*

legacy

If I was remembered for one poem,
I would want it to be like this one.
I would want the words to rain down on the audience;
        uplifting something within,
        causing a rebirth,
        a baptism of clauses
        like this one.
It would talk of the everlasting sunshine
        of joy,
Born from a slight brush of the hand,
        when given by the Gods of men
        to those who worship them,
        the plethora of ways melancholy
        can infect the soul,
        from mere heartache
        to extreme heartbreak;
        how the path can be strayed from
        due to these emotional earth quakes.
The rapid fire of love on one's heart,
        made even more unique
        due to its equally rapid end;
All these,
        made pure of their sorrow,
        or darkness,
        when looked at from the perspective
        of how short-lived their existence
A poem,
        that reminds us of all these things
        like this one
One that reflects,
        and analyzes
        to influence like this one.

An author, analyzes a narrator
        flaunting her character faults,
        the ever-present ability
        to drown in her own controversies
        instigating in her own problems,
        turning them into deadly daggers,
        aimed at all she holds dear.
A narrator
        reflects on the world that surrounds her;
        how the hate of her children,
        brings the deadly
        burning tears of Mother Earth
        while hands reach out, for that
        mysterious better horizon,
just
        one
        more
        inch
How the creative blossoms of the world,
        bloom later and later,
        until they bloom no longer,
New cultural advances seem to die
        under the repetition of old ones,
        leading us to our need
        to hold onto what we know
Is it really a psychotic notion
        to touch the unknown?
A poem
        that holds all these questions
        like this one
A poem,
        that holds out a miraculous hand,

to us Blind Men,
on our knees,
like this one,
Because within it
a tell-tale heart beats
the guilt,
the fear,
the madness of it all,
eating away at a soul so empty,
but surrounded by such fullness.
a fullness of others that can't penetrate
the Empty
A poem that describes the agony
of feeling alone,
when surrounded by so many:

A single lonely rose amidst so much vegetation,
like this one
A poem that drops the dime on these times
where religious controversies are the center
of conflict
because my religious beliefs are right
and yours are wrong
even though, we all get on our knees singing
the same song
to the sky, praying for better days
A poem
that didn't forget the streets
like this one
where one didn't know what was next to eat
because both mom and dad
are working 2 jobs to make rent and
pay for college tuition

because when you leave the house,
you will have a life worth living
not in the projects where they lived,
watching friends die
bullets breaking the windows with a crack
you had to sit on the floor
to eat again last night
that's why your back is all out of wack

A poem,

that gives respect,
where respect's due
like this one

All the people who sacrifice all they had
and more
for another to do better,
we thank you.

That's all the

mothers,
fathers,
aunts,
uncles,
brothers,
sisters,
grandmothers,
grandfathers,
friends,
homies,
cousins,
that random guy you met
at the street corner

That line is for you
A poem that also h o l l a s
at suburbia

where one gets lost one day
and found another.
So many paths to choose from,
in such open country
One day you're a boy, the next you're man
because you seem…
to begin…
to understand
the proper way to act
in certain society
That a girl is not
shorty
or baby
or hottie,
or some guy's sister
But a person that deserves the same respect
you would give your own sister
A poem
that expresses all these notions,
like this one
A poem that talks of the love a girl feels
for a boy who loves her back
Unfortunately,
he's going to fight in a war
she doesn't understand
and what she would give to keep her man,
here,
by her side
to take her hand
and be the guide
in the life they could have together,
But instead,
she's waving farewell to her lover,

from a window frame
and even now as we speak,
she's on her knees praying he comes home
in one piece
while he battles to bring about "more peace"
as he and his comrades sit in the desert
she prays
these desert flowers
don't get picked,
But safely return to their owners stateside.
a better prayer than this
she can't think of;
She is not the praying type
So instead,

she wrote out her thoughts in a poem,
which ran some pages like this one
beginning with the idea of a legacy,

"If I was remembered for one poem,
i would want it to be this one."

JOURNEY. DREAMS. TRANSFORMATION. THE PROCESS. NURTURING. CHA
VULNERABLE. METAMORPHOSIS. BEGINNING OF SOMETHING BEAUTIFUL
RENEWAL. JOURNEY. DREAMS. TRANSFORMATION. THE PROCESS. NURTU
STRUGGLE. VULNERABLE. METAMORPHOSIS. BEGINNING OF SOMETHING
TO HAPPEN. RENEWAL. JOURNEY. DREAMS. TRANSFORMATION. THE PROC
CHANGE. STRUGGLE. VULNERABLE. METAMORPHOSIS. BEGINNING OF SO
WAITING TO HAPPEN. RENEWAL. JOURNEY. DREAMS. TRANSFORMATION.
GROWTH. CHANGE. STRUGGLE. VULNERABLE. METAMORPHOSIS. BEG
METAMORPHOSIS WAITING TO HAPPEN. RENEWAL. JOURNEY. DREAMS.
PRE-ADULT STAGE. GROWTH. CHANGE. STRUGGLE. VULNERABLE. METAM
HUNGRY. METAMORPHOSIS WAITING TO HAPPEN. RENEWAL. JOURNEY. D
STAGE. PRE-ADULT STAGE. GROWTH. CHANGE. STRUGGLE. VULNERABLE.
VERY HUNGRY. METAMORPHOSIS WAITING TO HAPPEN. RENEWAL. JOUR
BABY STAGE. PRE-ADULT STAGE. GROWTH. CHANGE. STRUGGLE. VULN
CRAWLING. VERY HUNGRY. METAMORPHOSIS WAITING TO HAPPEN. RE
CATERPILLAR. BABY STAGE. PRE-ADULT STAGE. GROWTH. CHANGE. S
KINDERGARTEN. CRAWLING. VERY HUNGRY. METAMORPHOSIS WAITING T
CHANGE. CATERPILLAR. BABY STAGE. PRE-ADULT STAGE. GROWTH. CH
KINDERGARTEN. CRAWLING. VERY HUNGRY. METAMORPHOSIS WAITI
CHANGE. CATERPILLAR. BABY STAGE. PRE-ADULT STAGE. GROWTH. CH
KINDERGARTEN. CRAWLING. VERY HUNGRY. METAMORPHOSIS
CHANGE. CATERPILLAR. BABY STAGE. PRE-ADULT
BEAUTIFUL. KINDERGARTEN. CRAW
PROCESS. NURTURING. CHANGE. CATERPILLAR. BABY STAGE. PRE-
SOMETHING BEAUTIFUL. KINDERGARTEN. CRAWLING. VERY HU
THE PROCESS. NURTURING. CHANGE. CATERPILLAR. BABY STAGE. PRE
BEGINNING OF SOMETHING BEAUTIFUL. KINDERGARTEN. CRAWLING
TRANSFORMATION. THE PROCESS. NURTURING. CHANGE. CATERPILLA
METAMORPHOSIS. BEGINNING OF SOMETHING BEAUTIFUL. KINDERGA
JOURNEY. DREAMS. TRANSFORMATION. THE PROCESS. NURTURING. CH
VULNERABLE. METAMORPHOSIS. BEGINNING OF SOMETHING BEAUTIFU
RENEWAL. JOURNEY. DREAMS. TRANSFORMATION. THE PROCESS. NUR
STRUGGLE. VULNERABLE. METAMORPHOSIS. BEGINNING OF SOMETHIN
TO HAPPEN. RENEWAL. JOURNEY. DREAMS. TRANSFORMATION. THE PRO
CHANGE. STRUGGLE. VULNERABLE. METAMORPHOSIS. BEGINNING OF
WAITING TO HAPPEN. RENEWAL. JOURNEY. DREAMS. TRANSFORMATIO
GROWTH. CHANGE. STRUGGLE. VULNERABLE. METAMORPHOSIS. BE
METAMORPHOSIS WAITING TO HAPPEN. RENEWAL. JOURNEY. DREAMS
PRE-ADULT STAGE. GROWTH. CHANGE. STRUGGLE. VULNERABLE. META
HUNGRY. METAMORPHOSIS WAITING TO HAPPEN. RENEWAL. JOURNEY.
STAGE. PRE-ADULT STAGE. GROWTH. CHANGE. STRUGGLE. VULNERABLE
VERY HUNGRY. METAMORPHOSIS WAITING TO HAPPEN. RENEWAL. JOU
BABY STAGE. PRE-ADULT STAGE. STRUGGLE. VUL
CRAWLING. VERY HUNGRY. METAMORPHOSIS WAITING TO HAPPEN. R
CATERPILLAR. BABY STAGE. PRE-ADULT STAGE. GROWTH. CHANGE

PILLAR. BABY STAGE. PRE-ADULT STAGE. GROWTH. CHANGE. STRUGGL
RTEN. CRAWLING. VERY HUNGRY. METAMORPHOSIS WAITING TO HAPPE
NGE. CATERPILLAR. BABY STAGE. PRE-ADULT STAGE. GROWTH. CHANG
. KINDERGARTEN. CRAWLING. VERY HUNGRY. METAMORPHOSIS WAITIN
RING. CHANGE. CATERPILLAR. BABY STAGE. PRE-ADULT STAGE. GROWTI
EAUTIFUL. KINDERGARTEN. CRAWLING. VERY HUNGRY. METAMORPHOSI
SS. NURTURING. CHANGE. CATERPILLAR. BABY STAGE. PRE-ADULT STAG
SOMETHING BEAUTIFUL. KINDERGARTEN. CRAWLING. VERY HUNGR
ATION. THE PROCESS. NURTURING. CHANGE. CATERPILLAR. BABY STAG
EGINNING OF SOMETHING BEAUTIFUL. KINDERGARTEN. CRAWLING. VER
NSFORMATION. THE PROCESS. NURTURING. CHANGE. CATERPILLAR. BAB
OSIS. BEGINNING OF SOMETHING BEAUTIFUL. KINDERGARTEN. CRAWLING
. TRANSFORMATION. THE PROCESS. NURTURING. CHANGE. CATERPILLA
AMORPHOSIS. BEGINNING OF SOMETHING BEAUTIFUL. KINDERGARTE
NEY. DREAMS. TRANSFORMATION. THE PROCESS. NURTURING. CHANG
LNERABLE. METAMORPHOSIS. BEGINNING OF SOMETHING BEAUTIFU
NEWAL. JOURNEY. DREAMS. TRANSFORMATION. THE PROCESS. NURTURIN
. VULNERABLE. METAMORPHOSIS. BEGINNING OF SOMETHING BEAUTIFU
NEWAL. JOURNEY. DREAMS. TRANSFORMATION. THE PROCESS. NURTURIN
. VULNERABLE. METAMORPHOSIS. BEGINNING OF SOMETHING BEAUTIFU
NEWAL. JOURNEY. DREAMS. TRANSFORMATION. THE PROCESS. NURTURIN
UGGLE. VULNERABLE. METAMORPHOSIS. BEGINNING OF SOMETHIN
G TO HAPPEN. RENEWAL. JOURNEY. DREAMS. TRANSFORMATION. TH
TH. CHANGE. STRUGGLE. VULNERABLE. METAMORPHOSIS. BEGINNING O
S WAITING TO HAPPEN. RENEWAL. JOURNEY. DREAMS. TRANSFORMATIO
GROWTH. CHANGE. STRUGGLE. VULNERABLE. **LARVA** METAMORPHOSI
METAMORPHOSIS WAITING TO HAPPEN. RENEWAL. JOURNEY. DREAM
GE. PRE-ADULT STAGE. GROWTH. CHANGE. STRUGGLE. VULNERABL
NG. VERY HUNGRY. METAMORPHOSIS WAITING TO HAPPEN. RENEWA
LLAR. BABY STAGE. PRE-ADULT STAGE. GROWTH. CHANGE. STRUGGL
TEN. CRAWLING. VERY HUNGRY. METAMORPHOSIS WAITING TO HAPPE
GE. CATERPILLAR. BABY STAGE. PRE-ADULT STAGE. GROWTH. CHANG
KINDERGARTEN. CRAWLING. VERY HUNGRY. METAMORPHOSIS WAITIN
NG. CHANGE. CATERPILLAR. BABY STAGE. PRE-ADULT STAGE. GROWT
AUTIFUL. KINDERGARTEN. CRAWLING. VERY HUNGRY. METAMORPHOS
. NURTURING. CHANGE. CATERPILLAR. BABY STAGE. PRE-ADULT STAG
OMETHING BEAUTIFUL. KINDERGARTEN. CRAWLING. VERY HUNGR
ION. THE PROCESS. NURTURING. CHANGE. CATERPILLAR. BABY STAG
GINNING OF SOMETHING BEAUTIFUL. KINDERGARTEN. CRAWLING. VEI
FORMATION. THE PROCESS. NURTURING. CHANGE. CATERPILLAR. BAE
SIS. BEGINNING OF SOMETHING BEAUTIFUL. KINDERGARTEN. CRAWLIN
TRANSFORMATION. THE PROCESS. NURTURING. CHANGE. CATERPILLA
MORPHOSIS. BEGINNING OF SOMETHING BEAUTIFUL. KINDERGARTE
EY. DREAMS. TRANSFORMATION. THE PROCESS. NURTURING. CHANG
NERABLE. METAMORPHOSIS. BEGINNING OF SOMETHING BEAUTIFU

misled

You're the bottom of the food chain
You have to fight harder
You have to claw backs to get farther
According to my father
I have to be a killer and leave carcasses in the gutter
To be better
No wonder they are killing us in the street
Because we always go for each other's jugular to get ahead
But now and again
        a movement takes moments for harmony and strength
        put up a fist, take down a knee
        say how much i love my black and it loves me
Red, Black, and Green to bring my pride out of hiding
We out here trying to uplift and resist
        but that requires an understanding
        that still doesn't seem to exist
We all struggle but we all are different
We are all black but our denial is efficient
A coalition of children who never knew the siblings we needed
        in the Bronx
        in Brooklyn
        in Detroit
        in Chicago
        in LA

in the Carolinas
in Minneapolis
in Syria
in Lybia
in Palestine
Struggle invariant
Murder apparent
And inevitable
Tell me again how are we not brothers
and the concerns of others
isn't our business
Keep your head down
trouble won't be found
But we forgot
according to everyone else
the trouble is us
So tell me again how i get ahead
when my sister can't get fed
when my brother is misled
when my family's land is diplomatically seized
when my cousins died from pharmaceutical disease
Tell me again how i get ahead?
that isn't reminiscent of the people
who put me in my place to do the same?

nomad

Walk,
>run,
>ride,
>drive,
>fly

I cover thousands of miles in a blink of an
>eye

My home is here,
>there,
>everywhere
>and nowhere.

I get lost in tunnels and found on bridges,
>where sunlight can invade,
>beat back the gloom

Tunnels remind me of
>across the bridge I ride,
>ending at a platform
>where I walk-run to my next home

Where shall I go now?

For I am the Nomad.
>and no place is too far.

London Paris Cairo St. Petersburg
Hong Kong Tokyo Sydney Rome
San Fransisco Las Vegas Dallas
New Orleans Atlanta Memphis
DC State College Dover New York
>No place too far.

Amtrak NJ Transit Fullington Trailways Delta,
American Airlines Greyhound MTA
All my chariots to the better end.
>the better home.
>No ride too lowly,
>for I am the nomad.

Where shall I go?

sights

I walked through a white city
> that sat on brown red and green contours of an island
> that has survived centuries of man's mistakes

That was *humbling*.

love

The ocean parted for our boat
Cobalt blue and cereon danced around each other
Kissing the pure white suds as *they swirled by.*

sitting

Across the ocean is an island unnamed to me
It remains so still while my body shakes with the ships awakening
The wind picks up as we glide like a heron across the ocean
        away from the suns warmth
        but still witness to its strength
        lighting the unnamed island
        like mother nature's photography assistant
Perfect outlines
        on every contour
        of trees and hills, dive and cove
We turn and turn as a ballerina doing a slowed pirouette
Our balance held by our partner: the sea's salt
Which can be smelled on every new breeze
Which has lessened as we point in our next direction
I watch all this
        imprint it on my brain
        to describe it to you later
        so it can become *real for both of us.*

white man on a train

He held onto the pole with carefree grace
   leaning back,
   rocking one sneakered foot,
   disguising his rounded back as a stretch
Light blue pants with elastic band to fit his worn away waist
A pink undershirt gives color to a thin white button up
   giving his skin a touch of color that time has stolen
Clashing with the stark white hair
   he combs perfectly back without looking
A smooth killer
   coming between train cars
   where men, years his junior, would not dare
Old school
"I like your style, white man"
   who knows who we could've been in a previous life
With your style
   & my class
   the whole of New York as our playground…
   fun times perhaps
I wonder
   where you are going?
I wonder

   why you are alone?
   are you visiting someone?
   or, like me, do you just like to ride the train
   around your home?

school house rock
taught me

I'm just a bill
Yes, I'm only a bill
And I'm sitting here on capitol hill
        awaiting egotistical toddlers
        to stop playing this game of checkers
        with peoples lives
For the media
        to find its objective vocabulary
        instead of spewing propaganda bordering lies
If I hear "godfather esque" one more time!
        like faith in this government
        wasn't skewered and fried
        since Nixon's time
And for people of color,
        long before,
        when we removed the scales of
        disassociation from our eyes
I find it funny
        when I see a chick from Utah
        crying about her government induced woes
And it might be my New York insensibility
        that has a tendency to see the midwest
        as a giant blob
But I'm pretty sure she voted for him
        and that's judgey
But you see I'm a little angry
        at people crying 'whoa is me'
Where is the humanity
        that would dance on my grave
        if I was criminalized like Korynn Gaines
        or Assata
Who is *still living in Cuba.*

22

My body reminds me
> any moment it's ready
> to shut this shit down
> with a sharp sting in my side
> kidneys working overtime
> balancing medication and my (medicated) actions

I'm too busy shutting this party down
> to heed the warning
> whiskey & rum is flowing
> vodka shots on deck

What's the point of 22, if I can't flex?
> balloon disease riddled body
> has slimmed back down
> i'm living it up to take back
> 20 and 19
> right here, right now
> this night, these lights
> this place, these people
> his face, my lips
> his radiating touch

It is enough tonight...

tomorrow will be another story.

for a day

A touch, a dance forgotten
        but then again we meet
        and I no longer mind
        the slight shuffle of your feet
But instead,
        fall into your mesmerizing eyes
        because they see me
        not my breasts
        or my ass
        or the vision of me naked on your bed
But me
        so I let you have a piece of me
        because I know it won't hurt
The next day I gave a little more
        then a walk in the park
        allows me to give it all
        and like Whitney,
        i exhale over your shoulder
        cause you have allowed me to breathe
        and with certainty,
I can say…
        for a day
        I loved you.

nonsense

Lewis Carrol wrote nonsense so why can't I?
Jabberwocky was just a cry of insanity
        for a moment,
        from a mind that was under the influence
        of something
Some of the greatest work comes from those
        a little off their rocker
I mean
        would Lucy have flown with diamonds
        if Paul and John had been sober?

I. M. A. G. I. N. E.

I've never been high,
        but I've always wanted to try
        just to see what would happen…
I wonder if I'll go mad
        or be ingeniously inspired?
Will I get angry with a past offense
        or cry at my own loneliness?
Will my sexual prowess reveal herself
        or will I fold up deeper into myself?
I think of the last couplet, I prefer the latter
It may bring about a better understanding of myself
        or at least a deeper literary topic
Perhaps I won't feel anything at all
I'll make sure I have a pad nearby
        to tell you.

shaken

It winked in the bar lights
        dancing at the sight
        of me as it dangled
        in its master's hands
Oh the adventures it promised me!
        the thick brown slice that he called a brownie
        was more a slice of cake
I love cake
        vanilla more than chocolate
But i thought for such a specimen worth it
        to risk it
        my tastebuds,
        not my mental faculties
Bear with me
        i'll come back
I took a bite.
        soft, moist, baked,
        chocolate
        sitting under matching icing
        smelling of sugar and cocoa

Calling me
> to indulge in
> this evening
> in the shimmer
> of the drop of glaze left on my lips

I slowly lick
> mixing the test of possibility
> and my lemon lip gloss
> waiting for that nice feeling

When i feel nice
> i don't feel much so I take another bite
> melted on my tongue,
> hallucinogenic oil baked within
> blends with fluids in my mouth,
> a swirl of delectable dessert and
> underwhelm of effect

I don't feel much…
> so i take another bite.
> and another bite.
> and one more for good measure,
> because i'm feeling the pleasure
> of the music and the company,
> and it doesn't phase me,

The guy bugging next to me,
            who ate the same thing,
            and his warning,
            that a little will do ya...
            until a step outside, when my body shakes
            from the earth quake approach of the yellow cab
            that is felt behind my eyes
My mind can't decide
            what's real!
            because my heart is screaming danger of explosion
            but my mind doesn't hear any ticking
My chest is suddenly crushing it
            and my heart's need for adventure
My body feels like its jack hammer vibrating
            but my mind doesn't feel any thing slamming
            except my heart's war drums against its prison
Confusion has me drowning in this sensory pool
Alice must be best friends with Mary Jane
            because they supplanted Wonderland into me
Did I slip or did the sky fall?

Why does anyone go underground,
         aren't they also regarded senseless from the noise
Dragon rumbling that makes
         even your lungs hurt
Oh, there goes the war drums
         and now my brain is dancing in rhythm
A ritual to keep back the number of people strolling by
         like giants, GOD they walk so LOUDLY!
My eyes leak tears to release the
         pressure from my brains dancing
         and the rhythm keeps going and
         going and going and going
Should they name me the Energizer bunny?
Oh, laughter makes it worse
         and my boyfriend is just as in tune
         and just as confused
so we sit wrapped in each other at a bus stop
         until the wave *flows to someone else.*

truthful shorts

Alleviate the pressure of time
        by elevating my mind
        with the caress of your tongue

As I await the muse's touch,
        i touch myself;
Perhaps a song will come
        from the sensation.

Exhaustingly spoiled
        with compliments,
        lacking substance
You make promises
        you can't keep all the time!

The same that way,
        you and I...

double standard

It's always funny to me how often people joke
        of men's infidelities
        as if all women are angels in disguise
        heaven on Earth for the right eyes

There is no angel in this skin
        and if you look at the devil within
        she is the epitome of me
So when people say do you trust him?
        they should ask, does he trust you?

"He sees the God in me." I'd answer
"But neglects the rabid dog that lays down at Chaos' feet"

And before they take ill trying to make me feel better,
        a reminder comes from my lips
"Was it not the curiosity of Eve that led us out of the garden
        supposedly..allegedly?"

The thing about propaganda
        is that it's exaggerated and twisted truths,
        so when you unravel them,
        you unravel a little bit of your sanity too.

& as I am born
>from Eve's loins
>does that make me any better?
>is it not easy to slip into generational habits?

Curiosity is a funny thing
>without it we would still be sitting in great plains
>without flames eating raw meat
But with it we live
>with pain, great gains and more mistakes
>waiting at out feet

And then they say mistakes are lessons to make us better,
>"but where does that leave him?"
He who saw God in me,
>who trusted me,
>& is left with the ache of the hollowness
>left behind by mistakes...my mistakes?

How does a lesson help with the pain of destruction?

How does his new hardness affirm my actions?

How do you tell the *devil, she was right?*

relationships

Reason has nothing to do with it.
Emotional sexually fueled attraction, that's the core.
Later, romance is made the excusing explanation,
Always trying to make a personal fairytale.
That's not the whole truth though.
I never tried to do that, not with us.
Of course, I like you, but I could easily leave you,
No doubt in my mind.
Should we pretend this is more than a fling?
Honey lined lies never help anyone
I'd rather burn in desire and our truth.
Please, let's keep this simple.
Shamefully, but *sweetly simple.*

tale of 2 cities

Across the street
        are flip flops that walk to a Starbucks
        next to appropriated gold Nikes
        that the owner thought was
        so Brooklyn
Where I stand
        a woman walks past with old Ugg slippers
        shucking on concrete next to "like-new" Iverson's
Across the street
        oblivious little girls in jean jackets
        get pulled on three-wheel scooters
        to organic stores
        for banana chips
Where I stand
        oblivious little girl in a red down coat
        gets pulled while wearing matching red baby Jordan's
Somewhere in the middle
        a black man and a white man walk
        alongside each other;
        old friends

Somewhere in the middle,
        a tooth-losing man charges his smartphone
        at the new charging kiosk
Across the street,
        there's an organic market
        and 2 banks
Where I stand
        there's a check cashing,
        a Key Food,
        and the African market
Across the street,
        there's a newly opened juice shop
Where I stand
        there's a newly closed Jamaican shop
Somewhere in the middle
        a black girl with a fro-hawk, bikes to the
        Golden Krust
        for a chicken patty and coco bread
Somewhere in the middle,
        there's a crown
        fried chicken coffee shop

Across the street,
                    there's a newly renovated apartment I'd like to rent
Where I stand
                    is my grandfather's project apartment he's rented for
                    over 50 years
On either side,
                    i can't afford a place to live
On either side,
                    i'm afraid my bike will get stolen

Quiet comfort in consistencies
                    no matter how terrible
                    but then...
Somewhere in the middle
                    is a restaurant that serves creole brunch
Across the street
                    are newly planted trees
                    with green leaves reaching for the future
On my side of the street
                    are bare trees wearing Christmas decorations
                    made of plastic bags
                    worn all year round:

Across the street,
        there's a girl couple
        wearing Betty Boop attire
On my side of the street
        a couple of girls learning the hard way
        while wearing gold crosses and
        college sweatshirts
Somewhere in the middle
        is a revamped playground
        dedicated to Jackie Robinson
Somewhere in the middle
        is a public school and
        a charter school sharing the same building
Somewhere in the middle,
        a young, up-and-coming white couple
        walking out of the projects
Somewhere in the middle,
        i'm stumbling to *either side*.

HIBERNATION. WAITING. INACTIVE. SURVIVAL. WINTER. GROWTH. TRANSFO
NACTIVE. SURVIVAL. WINTER. GROWTH. TRANSFORMATION. CRADLE. SAF
WINTER. GROWTH. TRANSFORMATION. CRADLE. SAFETY. NURTURING. SL
TRANSFORMATION. CRADLE. SAFETY. NURTURING. SLEEP. REST. UNSURE.
CRADLE. SAFETY. NURTURING. SLEEP. REST. UNSURE. HIBERNATION. WAI
NURTURING. SLEEP. REST. UNSURE. HIBERNATION. WAITING. INACTIVE. SU
REST. UNSURE. HIBERNATION. WAITING. INACTIVE. SURVIVAL. WINTER.
HIBERNATION. WAITING. INACTIVE. SURVIVAL. WINTER. GROWTH. TRA
WAITING. INACTIVE. SURVIVAL. WINTER. GROWTH. TRANSFORMATION. CR
URVIVAL. WINTER. GROWTH. TRANSFORMATION. CRADLE. SAFETY.
WINTER. GROWTH. TRANSFORMATION. CRADLE. SAFETY. NURTURING. SL
TRANSFORMATION. CRADLE. SAFETY. NURTURING. SLEEP. REST. UNSURE.
CRADLE. SAFETY. NURTURING. SLEEP. REST. UNSURE. HIBERNATION. WA
NURTURING. SLEEP. REST. UNSURE. HIBERNATION. WAITING. INACTIVE. S
REST. UNSURE. HIBERNATION. WAITING. INACTIVE. SURVIVAL. WINTER
HIBERNATION. WAITING. INACTIVE. SURVIVAL. WINTER. GROWTH. TRA
WAITING. INACTIVE. SURVIVAL. WINTER. GROWTH. TRANSFORMATION. C
URVIVAL. WINTER. GROWTH. TRANSFORMATION. CRADLE. SAFETY.
WINTER. GROWTH. TRANSFORMATION. CRADLE. SAFETY. NURTURING.
RANSFORMATION. CRADLE. SAFETY. NURTURING. SLEEP. REST. UNSU
RADLE. SAFETY. NURTURING. SLEEP. REST. UNSURE. HIBERNATION.
AFETY. NURTURING. SLEEP. REST. UNSURE. HIBERNATION.
LEEP. REST. UNSURE. HIBERNATION.
IBERNATION. WAITING. INACTIVE. SURVIVAL. WINTER. GROWTH. TR
NACTIVE. SURVIVAL. WINTER. GROWTH. TRANSFORMATION. CRA
VINTER. GROWTH. TRANSFORMATION. CRADLE. SAFETY. NU
RANSFORMATION. CRADLE. SAFETY. NURTURING. SLEEP. REST. UR
RADLE. SAFETY. NURTURING. SLEEP. REST. UNSURE. IBERNATION. W
URTURING. SLEEP. REST. UNSURE. HIBERNATION. WAITING. INACTIVE
EST. UNSURE. HIBERNATION. WAITING. INACTIVE. SURVIVAL. INTE
IBERNATION. WAITING. INACTIVE. SURVIVAL. WINTER. GROWTH.
NACTIVE. SURVIVAL. WINTER. GROWTH. TRANSFORMATION. RADLE. SA
VINTER. GROWTH. TRANSFORMATION. CRADLE. SAFETY. NURTUR.
RANSFORMATION. CRADLE. SAFETY. NURTURING. SLEEP. REST. U SUR
RADLE. SAFETY. NURTURING. SLEEP. REST. UNSURE. HIBERNATIN. W
URTURING. SLEEP. REST. UNSURE. HIBERNATION. WAITING. INACTIVE.
EST. UNSURE. HIBERNATION. WAITING. INACTIVE. SURVIVAL. WINTE
IBERNATION. WAITING. INACTIVE. SURVIVAL. WINTER GROWTH. TRANS
NACTIVE. SURVIVAL. WINTER GROWTH. TRANSFORMATION. CRADLE. S
VINTER. GROWTH. TRANSFORMATION. CRADLE. SAFETY. NURTURING.
RANSFORMATION. CRADLE. SAFETY. NURTURING. SLEEP. REST. UNSUR
RADLE. SAFETY. NURTURING. SLEEP. REST. UNSURE. HIBERNATION. W
URTURING. SLEEP. REST. UNSURE. HIBERNATION. WAITING. INACTIVE.
EST. UNSURE. HIBERNATION. WAITING. INACTIVE. SURVIVAL. WINTE
IBERNATION. WAITING. INACTIVE. SURVIVAL. WINTER. GROWTH. TR

RADLE. SAFETY. NURTURING. SLEEP. REST. UNSURE. HIBERNATION. WAITING

RING. SLEEP. REST. UNSURE. HIBERNATION. WAITING. INACTIVE. SURVIVAL

NSURE. HIBERNATION. WAITING. INACTIVE. SURVIVAL. WINTER. GROWTH

N. WAITING. INACTIVE. SURVIVAL. WINTER. GROWTH. TRANSFORMATION

IVE. SURVIVAL. WINTER. GROWTH. TRANSFORMATION. CRADLE. SAFETY

NTER. GROWTH. TRANSFORMATION. CRADLE. SAFETY. NURTURING. SLEEP

RANSFORMATION. CRADLE. SAFETY. NURTURING. SLEEP. REST. UNSURE

N. CRADLE. SAFETY. NURTURING. SLEEP. REST. UNSURE. HIBERNATION

Y. NURTURING. SLEEP. REST. UNSURE. HIBERNATION. WAITING. INACTIVE

SLEEP. REST. UNSURE. HIBERNATION. WAITING. INACTIVE. SURVIVAL

NSURE. HIBERNATION. WAITING. INACTIVE. SURVIVAL. WINTER. GROWTH

N. WAITING. INACTIVE. SURVIVAL. WINTER. GROWTH. TRANSFORMATION

VE. SURVIVAL. WINTER. GROWTH. TRANSFORMATION. CRADLE. SAFETY

TER. GROWTH. TRANSFORMATION. CRADLE. SAFETY. NURTURING. SLEEP

ANSFORMATION. CRADLE. SAFETY. NURTURING. SLEEP. REST. UNSURE

N. CRADLE. SAFETY. NURTURING. SLEEP. REST. UNSURE. HIBERNATION

Y. NURTURING. SLEEP. REST. UNSURE. HIBERNATION. WAITING. INACTIVE

SLEEP. REST. UNSURE. HIBERNATION. WAITING. INACTIVE. SURVIVAL

SURE. HIBERNATION. WAITING. INACTIVE. SURVIVAL. WINTER. GROWTH

N. WAITING. INACTIVE. SURVIVAL. WINTER. GROWTH. TRANSFORMATION

E. SURVIVAL. WINTER. GROWTH. **CHRYSALIS**. TRANSFORMATION. CRADLE

AL. WINTER. GROWTH. TRANSFORMATION. CRADLE. SAFETY. NURTURING

TRANSFORMATION. CRADLE. SAFETY. NURTURING. SLEEP. REST. UNSURE

ADLE. SAFETY. NURTURING. SLEEP. REST. UNSURE. HIBERNATION. WAITING

NG. SLEEP. REST. UNSURE. HIBERNATION. WAITING. INACTIVE. SURVIVAL

SURE. HIBERNATION. WAITING. INACTIVE. SURVIVAL. WINTER. GROWTH

. WAITING. INACTIVE. SURVIVAL. WINTER. GROWTH. TRANSFORMATION

VE. SURVIVAL. WINTER. GROWTH. TRANSFORMATION. CRADLE. SAFETY

TER. GROWTH. TRANSFORMATION. CRADLE. SAFETY. NURTURING. SLEEP

ANSFORMATION. CRADLE. SAFETY. NURTURING. SLEEP. REST. UNSURE

ADLE. SAFETY. NURTURING. SLEEP. REST. UNSURE. HIBERNATION. WAITING

NG. SLEEP. REST. UNSURE. HIBERNATION. WAITING. INACTIVE. SURVIVA

SURE. HIBERNATION. WAITING. INACTIVE. SURVIVAL. WINTER. GROWTH

. WAITING. INACTIVE. SURVIVAL. WINTER. GROWTH. TRANSFORMATION

E. SURVIVAL. WINTER. GROWTH. TRANSFORMATION. CRADLE. SAFETY

ER. GROWTH. TRANSFORMATION. CRADLE. SAFETY. NURTURING. SLEEP

NSFORMATION. CRADLE. SAFETY. NURTURING. SLEEP. REST. UNSUR

DLE. SAFETY. NURTURING. SLEEP. REST. UNSURE. HIBERNATION. WAITING

NG. SLEEP. REST. UNSURE. HIBERNATION. WAITING. INACTIVE. SURVIVA

URE. HIBERNATION. WAITING. INACTIVE. SURVIVAL. WINTER. GROWTH

WAITING. INACTIVE. SURVIVAL. WINTER. GROWTH. TRANSFORMATION

E. SURVIVAL. WINTER. GROWTH. TRANSFORMATION. CRADLE. SAFETY

ER. GROWTH. TRANSFORMATION. CRADLE. SAFETY. NURTURING. SLEEP

NSFORMATION. CRADLE. SAFETY. NURTURING. SLEEP. REST. UNSUR

CRADLE. SAFETY. NURTURING. SLEEP. REST. UNSURE. HIBERNATION

trapped

I have to keep the television on,
        or the music on
        or keep moving back and forth in the apartment.
Otherwise, I can keep hearing…
EVERYTHING!
Does it ever shut up?
        the sirens
        the shouts
        the catcalls
        the hammering
        the honking
I never wished for silence so much.
I never thought
        the silence of forests could comfort
        a girl born and raised on the hardest streets
        known to man.
She had a taste of something better,
        and now the familiar hole
        is a torture chamber
        mastered by a population of 280,000
        that won't
        just
        stop.

Stop shouting

        stop shooting
        stop honking
        stop driving
        stop fighting
        stop selling
        stop hustling
        stop hammering
        stop watching
        stop questioning
        stop loving
        stop hating
        stop moving
        stop living

Just stop,

So I can have some silence!
But then everyone would be dead.
So instead,

I close the window.

trust

Trust me when I say,
I am my own destroyer.
It takes little time
        but much planning.
I design obstacles from wishful thinking,
        birth emotional missiles
        at the moment my mind closes to reason
I declare war on life
        from the hovel hope makes.
And when all is fought and done,
        i retreat to the nothing hope leaves.
Trust me when I say,
        i am my own executioner.
My death warrant signed by my pure need to please
        and every quickened step taken to another's arms,
        is less time for my life to be in my own "free" hands.
Flee, my free will does.
Leaving the most lowly subject
        on its knees
        at the mercy
        of a supposedly kind heart.
Trust me when I say,
        i am my own murderer,
        allowing the fiend in through a window
        left open by my own lust.
Lowering my defenses at the slightest
        touch from the hand,
        when I need them the most
The dagger:
        my own folly
The assailant:
        my mind
Trust me when I say
        i am *my own destroyer*....

25

Bald again
        lost again
        found again,
        in your arms,
Alarmed
        alert
        sick
        & recovering
Life hurts.
        lips revive me
        songs remind me
        my heart is carefree
        i am magic.
And all experiences
        define it
My spell book
        hooks and weaponize my truth
I am dangerous
        i am love
        i am broken
        i am healed
        i am nothing

        i am enough.

when will my reflection show

Mirrors are funny things
        they're supposed to show you,
        what's there,
        but I've caught myself staring
        at everything that's
        not there
The light bouncing to form the reflection
        must be from another dimension
        because I don't know who that is
        with the downcast eyes,
        and fading lips
She looks like she's dying
        sunken cheeks,
        eyes puffy
        like from crying
"My reflection always held a smile,"
I think to myself
        it's been a while

And I remember as time goes by
> i remember when I didn't ask why
> i threw the punches, I dodged the shots
> i was growing taller, no sight of a stop

And I remember when the world was mine
> the golden path was laid at my feet
> there was no stopping the power
> that was all from me

but I look in the mirror
> and I don't know that face
> she looks familiar
> like there's a trace
> of a triumphant smile
> that I know I wore

I say it's been a while
> to this *mnemonic girl.*

clarity

Thoughts burrow holes in my brain
So deep that extraction requires annihilation of cognitive thought,
    vegetable status allowing clarity
No longer restricted by the image of the person I'm meant to be
Expectations are irrelevant
    when you're floating
    weightless, lifeless,
    soulful & awake
Don't mistake this escape
    as a call for bodily harm
I.

    just.
    need.
    a.
    second.
    to tell me to be quiet and mean it
I just need a moment
    to choke and not swallow
    on the hypocritical cum skeeted at me
    out of disrespect of my humanity
Tomorrow i could be a hashtag
    and all I'll have to show for it is this box in my head
    of who i was supposed to be
    a series of cookie cutter jobs that overexposed me
    a pile of papers that overcame me
    wrists dripping in ink
    fingers clacking in sync
    (i can type 175 words per minute)
    the faster to lose my light my dear
Eyes paled by fear
    cheeks vaguely smeared
    with words never said
    lifeblood spilling from the tip
    so i can scribble down this,
Some notes that got Out when i allowed myself some clarity

        after telling myself to shut up!

what's your type?

I heard a man once speak
    of a beautiful love between him,
    a woman
    and God.
A pure love with respect,
    understanding,
    and patience.

Where sex was a gift
    and not a necessity.
The man
    and the woman
    saw each other through God's eyes.
I am not that woman.
I am selfish and self-conscious.
I notice your faults,
    think of how to change them
    without telling you
I let other people influence me
    and thus our relationship
I see you through everyone else's eyes
    instead of my heart's

If I did
    i am afraid I will blind myself.
Instead of God's love,
    i would have the devil's obsession
    and *we would both go up in flames.*

ashes

It all went up in flames
Unexpected combustion
That still affects how i function
And there's nowhere to put in a claim
No one to whom i can complain
Life plans in ashes`
Because life's hand delivers lashes
To ensure you're in the right lane

A test of my tenacity
That I'm still not sure i passed
What will come of me?
A diseased dreamer with realistic tendencies
That stutters when asked
                of future plans,
                after my *Phoenix rises blindly.*

i can't

I can't think, I can't walk,
I can't eat, I can't write,
I can't cook, I can't sleep,
I can't drink, I can't dance,
I can't jump, I can't run,
I can't travel, I can't...

I can't remember when everything was not swollen,
I can't remember when there weren't ailments,
I can't remember when there weren't water balloons,
I can't remember when there weren't patterns.
I can't...

I can't sing, I can't design,
I can't drive, I can't play guitar,
I can't paint, I can't sew,
I can't plant, I can't mold,
I can't stitch, I can't...

Well, I couldn't actually do those before
but now I really can't!

I couldn't really cry, and now I can't stop.
I didn't really believe and now, how can I not?
I took it all for granted; now I can't.
What's it all for?
I didn't know the answer, now I can't stop obsessing over it.
>   questions of my existence dance
>   swirling circle in my head
>   i never know the steps now
I am obsessed and I can't stop dancing
I can't...

I can't make my hair grow back, I just have to wait.
I can't quick-heal my kidneys, I just have to take my meds.
I can't make time slow down, I just have to catch up.
I can't always smile.
I can't...

And *you can't always expect me to.*

a little less tanka
a little more touch my body

My leather jacket
            smells like me, comfortingly
            even sans perfume

A loving constant
            your fried chicken smelling shirt
            there in my closet

Faces come closer
            publicly than privately
            reminding whispers

Shall I grow for you?
            make myself the envision
            of a wed lady?

I'd rather get lost
            in the waves of nasty thoughts
            seducing myself

He pats my thigh
            while I tap the table,
            both pretending we didn't just strip the other
            with our mind,
Felt our bare pelvises grind;
            or our wet lips on brown necks
            lick desire, passion & sweat.

His hand grabbed my ass
        like he always wanted to,
My teeth bit his neck
        like they were always meant to.
He picked me up,
        to bring me down
        to the floor,
Cold linoleum on my back,
        balanced with his warmth on top.
Next his mouth enveloped my nipple
        from right
        to left
        then both,
His hands held them closer to his mouth
        as he massaged them on the side.
I moaned out pleasure
        and frustration
        at this sensual teasing sensation!
His hand traced a path down my stomach,
        to the inside of my thigh.
His mouth faithfully followed
        to my dismay & my desire.
And then he looked up into my eyes.
        and we both realized…

he was just patting my thigh,
and I was tapping the table.

healthy dosage

I can't escape you,
           but right now I don't want to.
The essence of your presence
           creates a euphoric aura around me.
Your smell lingers in my clothes;
           hours later I still feel your last embrace
And every time you turn to walk away
           I turn to outrun the heartache
Latching on
           until I see your face again,
           or hear your voice
           or feel your touch.
For me,
           love is not a sickness,
           but a nutrient my body needs
           in a healthy dose of 162 lbs,
Every second
           on the second
           of everyday….
But in the back of my mind,
           an anxious thought runs
           as steadily as Beethoven's 5th symphony
           (dun dun dun dun)
           preventing me from truly relaxing,
           from truly trusting this nutrient

I'm doubting its healthy attributes.
What if I'm the playboy bunny
            who thinks cocaine is good for her?
What if this nutrient makes my body
            dependent on it
            and then suddenly disappears?
Will my organs fail?
Will my skin pigment change?
My tear ducts, will they dry out?
Will I lose the desire to eat or drink or laugh?
Will I have nausea?
My mood, will it swing?
Please,
            someone tell me
            the effects of love deprivation
            and if one can survive!
Can I survive without my dose?
Or should I decrease it to every minute,
            every other day
            lessening the possible repercussions
            of a sudden lack of dosage?
A slow and steady beat these words form,
            undetectable in my subconscious
            because there hasn't been a lack of dosage
            and there's *a euphoric aura around me...*

scorched

When you grabbed the back of my neck
Pulled me to the wall
To bring your nose
                a whisper length from mine
My knees buckled in anticipation
I felt the gates flood
                at the release of their tether:
                sexual tension
My lips parted,
                subtle seduction
                like the girl in the pearl earring
This girl in the disappearing clothes
Questioned your next action
Then your tongue burrowed its way into my mouth
My eyes rolled back and I burned

satisfyingly scorched.

thorn

Blood trickles along our brown skin
From me to the thorn and back again
Blood promises always stand strong
Life was breathed into them
From your strength and my gasp
As you stabbed deep and true
Now your touch is embedded in skin's memories
Violent for one, intoxicating for the other
After all, your love has always been

the best thorn in my side.

trusting

You said to trust you
I'll let you have your cake
        and eat it too
My daddy didn't raise no sucker
        and I knew it too good to be true
But See
        my mistake lay
        in underestimating
        how royally fucked up was your inner you!
You got excuses
        for your excuses
        for your excuses
And when that doesn't keep me at bay
        you have plenty of papers to push my way
        with fine print
        chaining me into a gang
I thought higher education
        was supposed to elevate
I thought teachers of color were needed
        to make lessons relate
Wasn't that the purpose of the "Diversity in Education" class
        you made me pay for?

Or is it only about the quotas?
But I guess Times' sway will make even that go away
But you got this last fool to trust you
I didn't see where my American Dream went
                from a white picket fence
                to just living debt free
                in my momma's house

I didn't know Las Vegas
                changed its name to
                Department of Education
I ain't never gambled this much in my life!
My
                whole
                                        life

I bet on that roulette
                that you presented
                as a bank deposit
                or at least an investment

But they don't always *pan out.*

a series of truthful shorts

When I was 17
We drove with no hands
            and knew exactly what we wanted
Now I'm 27,
            hands firmly on the wheel
            with no idea what direction to head
And I'm told this is progress

Sometimes I hide out in my bedroom
            when I know I need to go to the kitchen
            to avoid possibly,
            bumping into my family,
            who also live here.

Privilege is
            debating to Netflix and Chill
            at his place or your place,
            on a tablet or computer,
            near a couple arguing about $20,
            while their baby cries *for food in a Taco Bell.*

changes

The limestone stoop is metal now
       and the old black man,
       who used to run the corner deli
       is long dead.
They even fixed the crooked steps
       that required a healthy exposure
       and some scraped knees to master.
I still hear my grandfather's voice,
       echoing in between my gasping
       as I walked the six flights
       to his Guyanese accent.

He used to call me 'Nickelodeon.'

The sidewalk is less foreboding,
       but it's also lost its shine,
Or maybe that's that haze of time
       lifting rose colored washing on my memories
And I finally get to see the beauty
       of the ghetto fabulous *that raised me.*

brown

Brown is not the most celebrated color
        but when I'm with him
        brown is all there is
As he calls me by my name:
        brown eyes
        while his brown hands
        guide my brown thighs
        around his strong waist

I caress his brown cheek
        as our brown lips
        envelope each other
        under his brown fitted,
        hanging on the wall
        near his favorite brown hoodie
        lying on the floor
I get all wrapped up in his melanin
        a felon in the rapture of his prison lock arms.
There I healed his heart,
        with the passion from mine.
There he rehabilitated my faith,
        with the strength of his.
What's worth more than that?

Now brown hands,
        grope red hearts,
        no need for smart tech
        for brown bodies to talk
We Radiate
        his pink tongue on my brown love
        makes for the perfect mix
Brown noses nuzzled in brown necks
        make for the perfect fix
That sensual feel is better than any sexual appeal
I love the way he smells
        as I fall deeper into his brown arms
        and a chill rolls down my brown back
I excitedly get all tangled up in our beautiful dark
        and like Ms. Arie
        I don't know which part is him
        and which is me

What I do know,
        is brown is not,
        the most celebrated color.
But when I'm with him,
        brown is all there is.

MIGRATE. CHANGES. BEGINNINGS. POSSIBILITIES. WITHOUT CHAINS.
BEAUTIFUL. ENDLESS. FREEDOM. RENEWING. OPENING. FREE. TR
CHANGE. BEGINNINGS. POSSIBILITIES. WITHOUT CHAINS. WITHOUT E
ENDLESS. FREEDOM. RENEWING. OPENING. FREE. TRANSFORMAT
BEGINNINGS. POSSIBILITIES. WITHOUT CHAINS. WITHOUT BOUNDARIES.
FREEDOM. RENEWING. OPENING. FREE. TRANSFORMATION. NATURE.
POSSIBILITIES. WITHOUT CHAINS. WITHOUT BOUNDARIES. FLYING. ASC
RENEWING. OPENING. FREE. TRANSFORMATION. NATURE. WITHOUT RE
WITHOUT CHAINS. WITHOUT BOUNDARIES. FLYING. ASCENDING. NAT
OPENING. FREE. TRANSFORMATION. NATURE. WITHOUT RESTRICTIONS
CHAINS. WITHOUT BOUNDARIES. FLYING. ASCENDING. NATURE. COLORF
TRANSFORMATION. NATURE. WITHOUT RESTRICTIONS. REBIRTH. STREN
BOUNDARIES. FLYING. ASCENDING. NATURE. COLORFUL SMILE. SPREAD.
NATURE. WITHOUT RESTRICTIONS. REBIRTH. STRENGTH. MIGRATE. CHA
ASCENDING. NATURE. COLORFUL SMILE. SPREAD. BEAUTIFUL. ENDLES
RESTRICTIONS. REBIRTH. STRENGTH. MIGRATE. CHANGES. BEGINNING
NATURE. COLORFUL SMILE. SPREAD. BEAUTIFUL. ENDLESSNESS. FREED
REBIRTH. STRENGTH. MIGRATE. CHANGES. BEGINNINGS. POSSIBILITIES
SMILE. SPREAD. BEAUTIFUL. ENDLESSNESS. FREEDOM. RENEWING
MIGRATE. CHANGES. BEGINNINGS. POSSIBILITIES. WITHOUT CHAINS
BEAUTIFUL. ENDLESSNESS. FREEDOM. RENEWING. OPENING
CHANGES. BEGINNINGS. POSSIBILITIES. WITHOUT
ENDLESSNESS. FREEDOM. RENEWING
BEGINNINGS. POSSIBILITIES. WITHOUT CHAINS. WITHOUT BOUN
FREEDOM. RENEWING. OPENING. FREE. TRANSFORMATION. NAT
POSSIBILITIES. WITHOUT CHAINS. WITHOUT BOUNDARIES. FLYING. A
RENEWING. OPENING. FREE. TRANSFORMATION. NATURE. WITHOUT R
WITHOUT CHAINS. WITHOUT BOUNDARIES. FLYING. ASCENDING. NATU
FREE. TRANSFORMATION. NATURE. WITHOUT RESTRICTIONS. REBIRTH
BOUNDARIES. FLYING. ASCENDING. NATURE. COLORFUL SMILE. SPRE
NATURE. WITHOUT RESTRICTIONS. REBIRTH. STRENGTH. MIGRA
ASCENDING. NATURE. COLORFUL SMILE. SPREAD. BEAUTIFUL. ENDLE
RESTRICTIONS. REBIRTH. STRENGTH. MIGRATE. CHANGES. BEGINNINGS.
COLORFUL SMILE. SPREAD. BEAUTIFUL. ENDLESSNESS. FREEDOM. REN
STRENGTH. MIGRATE. CHANGES. BEGINNINGS. POSSIBILITIES. WITHO
SPREAD. BEAUTIFUL. ENDLESSNESS. FREEDOM. RENEWING. OPENING. FR
CHANGES. BEGINNINGS. POSSIBILITIES. WITHOUT CHAINS. WITHOUT
ENDLESSNESS. FREEDOM. RENEWING. OPENING. FREE. TRANSFORM
BEGINNINGS. POSSIBILITIES. WITHOUT CHAINS. WITHOUT BOUNDARIE
FREEDOM. RENEWING. OPENING. FREE. TRANSFORMATION. NATURE
POSSIBILITIES. WITHOUT CHAINS. WITHOUT BOUNDARIES. FLYING. A
RENEWING. OPENING. FREE. TRANSFORMATION. NATURE. WITHOUT
WITHOUT CHAINS. WITHOUT BOUNDARIES. FLYING. ASCENDING. NATUR
FREE. TRANSFORMATION. NATURE. WITHOUT RESTRICTIONS. REBIRTH.
BOUNDARIES. FLYING. ASCENDING. NATURE. COLORFUL SMILE. SPREA

BOUNDARIES. FLYING. ASCENDING. NATURE. COLORFUL. SMILE. SPREAD
TION. NATURE. WITHOUT RESTRICTIONS. REBIRTH. STRENGTH. MIGRAT
, FLYING. ASCENDING. NATURE. COLORFUL SMILE. SPREAD. BEAUTIFU
E. WITHOUT RESTRICTIONS. REBIRTH. STRENGTH. MIGRATE. CHANGE
ENDING. NATURE. COLORFUL SMILE. SPREAD. BEAUTIFUL. ENDLESSNES
ESTRICTIONS. REBIRTH. STRENGTH. MIGRATE. CHANGES. BEGINNING
TURE. COLORFUL SMILE. SPREAD. BEAUTIFUL. ENDLESSNESS. FREEDOM
REBIRTH. STRENGTH. MIGRATE. CHANGES. BEGINNINGS. POSSIBILITIE
UL SMILE. SPREAD. BEAUTIFUL. ENDLESSNESS. FREEDOM. RENEWING
TRENGTH. MIGRATE. CHANGES. BEGINNINGS. POSSIBILITIES. WITHOU
READ. BEAUTIFUL. ENDLESSNESS. FREEDOM. RENEWING. OPENING. FRE
E. CHANGES. BEGINNINGS. POSSIBILITIES. WITHOUT CHAINS. WITHOU
ENDLESSNESS. FREEDOM. RENEWING. OPENING. FREE. TRANSFORMATIO
INGS. POSSIBILITIES. WITHOUT CHAINS. WITHOUT BOUNDARIES. FLYIN
OM. RENEWING. OPENING. FREE. TRANSFORMATION. NATURE. WITHOU
TIES. WITHOUT CHAINS. WITHOUT BOUNDARIES. FLYING. ASCENDIN
G. OPENING. FREE. TRANSFORMATION. NATURE. WITHOUT RESTRICTION
AINS. WITHOUT BOUNDARIES. FLYING. ASCENDING. NATURE. COLORFU
ANSFORMATION. NATURE. WITHOUT RESTRICTIONS. REBIRTH. STRENGT
UNDARIES. FLYING. ASCENDING. NATURE. COLORFUL SMILE. SPREA
ON. NATURE. WITHOUT RESTRICTIONS. REBIRTH. STRENGTH. MIGRAT
FLYING. ASCENDING. NATURE. COLORFUL SMILE. SPREAD. BEAUTIFU
E. WITHOUT RESTRICTIONS. REBIRTH. STRENGTH. MIGRATE. CHANGE
N. NATURE. COLORFUL SMILE. SPREAD. BEAUTIFUL. ENDLESSNES
REBIRTH. STRENGTH. MIGRATE. CHANGES. **WINGED** BEGINNING
UL SMILE. SPREAD. BEAUTIFUL. ENDLESSNESS. FREEDOM
EBIRTH. STRENGTH. MIGRATE. CHANGES. BEGINNINGS. POSSIBILITIE
TE. SPREAD. BEAUTIFUL. ENDLESSNESS. FREEDOM. RENEWING. OPENIN
ATE. CHANGES. BEGINNINGS. POSSIBILITIES. WITHOUT CHAINS. WITHOU
ENDLESSNESS. FREEDOM. RENEWING. OPENING. FREE. TRANSFORMATIO
INGS. POSSIBILITIES. WITHOUT CHAINS. WITHOUT BOUNDARIES. FLYIN
OM. RENEWING. OPENING. FREE. TRANSFORMATION. NATURE. WITHOU
WITHOUT CHAINS. WITHOUT BOUNDARIES. FLYING. ASCENDING. NATUR
E. FREE. TRANSFORMATION. NATURE. WITHOUT RESTRICTIONS. REBIRT
THOUT BOUNDARIES. FLYING. ASCENDING. NATURE. COLORFUL SMIL
ATION. NATURE. WITHOUT RESTRICTIONS. REBIRTH. STRENGTH. MIGRAT
FLYING. ASCENDING. NATURE. COLORFUL SMILE. SPREAD. BEAUTIFU
WITHOUT RESTRICTIONS. REBIRTH. STRENGTH. MIGRATE. CHANGE
NDING. NATURE. COLORFUL SMILE. SPREAD. BEAUTIFUL. ENDLESSNES
TRICTIONS. REBIRTH. STRENGTH. MIGRATE. CHANGES. BEGINNING
RE. COLORFUL SMILE. SPREAD. BEAUTIFUL. ENDLESSNESS. FREEDO
EBIRTH. STRENGTH. MIGRATE. CHANGES. BEGINNINGS. POSSIBILITIE
LE. SPREAD. BEAUTIFUL. ENDLESSNESS. FREEDOM. RENEWING. OPENIN
TE. CHANGES. BEGINNINGS. POSSIBILITIES. WITHOUT CHAINS. WITHOU
DLESSNESS. FREEDOM. RENEWING. OPENING. FREE. TRANSFORMATIO

rooms

We are emptying rooms slowly
            the shuffles of your feet I can still hear

Your shuffling feet, once so near, i still hear
            it fills the silence, your presence left

The silence screams in the void your presence left
            it's cold where your body once hummed
            with your voice

My body cold, where you once hummed with your voice,
            accepting silence better than ghostly notes

Can't leave you in the silence as ghostly notes
            but my heart has trouble resisting the screams

My heart's memories soothes the screams
            that in these new views of old rooms nothing's lost

new views of old rooms stirs memories thought lost
            my heart newly full as *rooms slowly empty.*

faith check in

Faith by definition is
> the complete trust or confidence
> in someone or something.

I have faith,
> in the common sense
> of the American populace,
> and our ability to tap into the power
> embedded in our mass....
> that will kick in at any moment...

I have faith,
> that our politicians
> will fuck up our nation further,
> before they fully fix it
> leading to a pseudo-golden age.

I have faith,
> in the fact that
> racism and prejudice
> are still the foundations of this nation's laws,
> but that others have realized this too,
> are trying to make a change,
> and they will eventually fail.

I have faith,
> in the conclusion
> that cell phones for my generation
> are cigarettes for my parents:
> a social blockade;
> and the rumor that they cause cancer
> will be made a fact in a decade

when we'll decrease our usage…
too little too late…

I have faith,

in God and how fucked up he can be,
and the blessings he does bestow.
we have a love-hate relationship,
but all true loves do
for good measure.

I have faith,

in the blessing God bestowed on me,
in the shape of a man,
who loves me against all sense or reason,
and gave me the sense to love him back,
until whatever miserable end is our destiny;
and *most likely long after that…*

need you

It's not that I'm not strong
It's not that I'm not sometimes wrong
It's not that I can't get along
I just need you

I can walk on my own
I can find my way home
I don't need someone to hold my hand
I just need you

It's not that things are really hard
It's not that I feel I need to always be on my guard
It's not that I now feel weak, and need someone to understand
I just need you

I can do my work just fine
I don't need a dime
I can get all I need to financially succeed
I just need you

It's not that I can't breathe when you're away
It's not that I feel lost when you don't stay

It's not that when you leave, to the darkness I concede
I just need you

And that's really hard for me to say
For it was a pride of mine, in a way
To not need you

But I do

I can't explain why you make me feel so relaxed
Why your words make the nightmares step back.
For a long time, I took care of myself
Your presence was not needed, and I had no doubt

In my abilities, years of practice had perfected
But now, I need you

And you don't have to do
Anything
Just stand there
Just be there
I just need you.

contracts

We're all bound up in something.
Pressuring us
Sometimes,
              to be nothing
So why not
              make these wraps
              work for us
Make them tighten
              to keep you calm
Make them loosen
              to help you grow
Choose them as carefully
              as you choose your regrets
But with as much love
              as you choose your
              favorite band-aid

To cover the scars
              these wraps will heal
              then you'll see what I see

A world where we all breath free
A world we all can be
A world where we appreciate the cracks,
              and the breaks and the discomfort
We honor the strengths, the dreams, and our voices
Shifters showing up, urgently loving humble power,
              trusting vulnerability, responsible risk-taking,
              and giving *authentic joy.*

beach

A water bottle
A seagull
Haloed clouds
              over 2 lovers
              standing next to their white car
A dog and his owner is startled
              by noise 'we call music' played by a passing driver
Cyclists
Bicyclists
Joggers
Walkers
Fun seekers

A girl shouts at a boy's
              obnoxious whistle
An ice cream family
              that moves in synchrony
A baby cries near older ladies
              who sigh over work frustrations
Green sneakers
              move swiftly under stiff shoulders while passing

The Lifeguard "off duty" sign
White tower snuggles
            with beige sand
As black rocks
            make new friends
            with daredevils
            Gangs
            Cliques
            Squads
            Crews
            Barefoot girl
            unsure of what to do
Shoes or no shoes?
Sizzling cold showers
Beaching after hours
Sherlock & Watson patrol the boardwalk
Drake plays off in the distance
As my inner teen gets in
            the last of her
            summer riches.

28

That moment when you realize
        the phrase
        "grown-up"
        was an illusion that too many people
        attempted to master as reality
A freedom is birthed
A breath releases
A path at my feet,
A choice not settling.

I will have my cake *and eat it too.*

the cake

I bled out my insecurities
Until i became faint with the wisdom
                that i don't know anything
And that's ok
This piece of paper says otherwise
And I'll make *my way.*

support

Lost in the throes of enlightenment
I climbed to fall
            into supportive hands
            that I've kept waiting for *far too long.*

dedication

They say I must have a lot of discipline
          and dedication
          to get this far
They say I must be a fighter
          to attempt to make my future brighter
          with this degree
Which I don't disagree,
          but it's the dedication
          that hits home for me
Dedication to these books.
Dedication to these classes.
Dedication to these evals that took hours.
Dedication to deadlines
          that at times
          might have been more fluid
          than originally agreed.
Dedication to a promise
          that I made to my past self;
          of, 'oh, all the places I would go'
          and the people I would meet.
Dedication to all my future feats.

See I wasn't supposed to get this far.
          according to what society told me,
But I did anyway
          and met some great people
          along the way

We shared sleepless nights
            and tear filled mornings
We shared comedic highlights
            and food scavenged from parties
We shared our success
            and comforted setbacks
We made a second family
            to combat
            the weight of dedication
            to fulfill dreams
Which leads me to my dedication
            to those who sacrificed in dedication to us

            Mothers,
            fathers,
            sisters,
            brothers,
            cousins,
            aunts,
            uncles,
            grandmothers,
            grandfathers,
            significant others,
            friends and professors
            Couples looking for someone
            to match their hustle
Well, y'all matched my dedication
            and I will *forever honor you for that.*

nana

3 days ago my grandmother passed away…
            and I've been searching for something to say;
But secrets and lies keep getting in the way.
We weren't close.
            but she challenged me just the same,
And I loved her for it in every way.
            even though petty animosity
            sometimes got in the way.
Acidic words hurled my way,
            had a knack for slipping back to her feet,
            but we found common ground where'd we
            sometimes meet
And laugh;
All the way to the day she passed.
And I sometimes ask:
"What was her name?"
I know what was written on her certificate,
            and what her friends called her.
But when she spoke to herself;
When she made decisions to hurt or help,
            what did she whisper?
Was it Dean or Hardenia?
Was it baby girl or honey?
Was it a nickname my Aunt Bunchie gave her
            that no one knew but them?
Was it a term of endearment from my grandfather
            or a previous lover we never met?
Or did she never use a name at all,
            when making entries to her mental diary?
Marking the moments of joy and drudgery,
Did she ever reprimand herself when she spouted venom?
Did she regret it?
Was she as lost as her daughters when she left them in Virginia?
Did she mourn the broken trust
            that was found between them, on reuniting?
Was she as elated as I, when she met the man
            she was destined to spend the rest of his life with?

Did she whisper, "Dean this is it?"
    and smiled to herself as her heart soared.
Did she haphazardly put a web around her daughters
    that kept them stuck but never together?
Or was she as conniving as the way we portray spiders?

She bought me underwear every Christmas!
Was it because she was lovingly practical
    or thought me pointedly undeserving?
But I guess she would have thought that of us all;
Because ALL the grandchildren got underwear EVERY YEAR.

But there was something about that box;
That red Macy's box that made you feel
    that even though everyone got the same
    this one was a unique shot at you
Or maybe that was just because it came from her hand…
Man,
    I didn't really know her that much at all.
She wasn't much of a talker, and I wasn't pressed to call.
But I'll say this: it doesn't really matter.
Because in her hospital bed she held on to my hand.
    then, she let me clip and paint her nails,
    where she fought with everyone else.
She had a witty comment for all my sass.
    and although she was dying, I didn't let pass
    the chance to be as we always were.

I didn't know her,
Very well,
But maybe, just maybe,
    the name she used to whisper to herself was "Nana."
Maybe it was always her favorite;
And that's why
    she had her grandchildren *call her that.*

momentum

I flowed along the stream of broken promises
               until I drowned on the rapids of my lies
I was revived by the sound of a truth I already knew
I am fulfilled
By the words, I've written and the ones yet known
I am fulfilled
And this quill
In *my hand is all I need.*

BUTTERFLY BUTTERFLY. BUTTERFLY BUTTERFLY. BUTTERFLY BUTTERFLY.
BUTTERFLY. BUTTERFLY BUTTERFLY. BUTTERFLY BUTTERFLY. BUTTERFLY
BUTTERFLY BUTTERFLY. BUTTERFLY BUTTERFLY. BUTTERFLY BUTTERFLY.
BUTTERFLY. BUTTERFLY BUTTERFLY. BUTTERFLY BUTTERFLY. BUTTERFLY
BUTTERFLY BUTTERFLY. BUTTERFLY BUTTERFLY. BUTTERFLY BUTTERFLY
BUTTERFLY. BUTTERFLY BUTTERFLY. BUTTERFLY BUTTERFLY. BUTTERFLY
BUTTERFLY BUTTERFLY. BUTTERFLY BUTTERFLY. BUTTERFLY BUTTERFLY
BUTTERFLY. BUTTERFLY BUTTERFLY. BUTTERFLY BUTTERFLY. BUTTERFLY
BUTTERFLY BUTTERFLY. BUTTERFLY BUTTERFLY. BUTTERFLY BUTTERFLY
BUTTERFLY. BUTTERFLY BUTTERFLY. BUTTERFLY BUTTERFLY. BUTTERFLY
BUTTERFLY BUTTERFLY. BUTTERFLY BUTTERFLY. BUTTERFLY BUTTERFLY
BUTTERFLY. BUTTERFLY BUTTERFLY. BUTTERFLY BUTTERFLY. BUTTERFLY
BUTTERFLY BUTTERFLY. BUTTERFLY BUTTERFLY. BUTTERFLY BUTTERFLY
BUTTERFLY. BUTTERFLY BUTTERFLY. BUTTERFLY BUTTERFLY. BUTTERFLY
BUTTERFLY BUTTERFLY. BUTTERFLY BUTTERFLY. BUTTERFLY BUTTERFLY
BUTTERFLY. BUTTERFLY BUTTERFLY. BUTTERFLY BUTTERFLY. BUTTERFL
BUTTERFLY BUTTERFLY. BUTTERFLY BUTTERFLY. BUTTERFLY BUTTERFL
BUTTERFLY. BUTTERFLY BUTTERFLY. BUTTERFLY BUTTERFLY. BUTTERFL
BUTTERFLY. BUTTERFLY **AFTERWORDS**. BUTTERFLY. BUTTERFLY BUTTERF
BUTTERFLY. BUTTERFLY BUTTERFLY. BUTTERFLY BUTTERFLY. BUTTERFL
BUTTERFLY BUTTERFLY. BUTTERFLY BUTTERFLY. BUTTERFLY BUTTERFL
BUTTERFLY. BUTTERFLY BUTTERFLY. BUTTERFLY BUTTERFLY. BUTTERFL
BUTTERFLY BUTTERFLY. BUTTERFLY BUTTERFLY. BUTTERFLY BUTTERFL
BUTTERFLY. BUTTERFLY BUTTERFLY. BUTTERFLY BUTTERFLY. BUTTERFI
BUTTERFLY BUTTERFLY. BUTTERFLY BUTTERFLY. BUTTERFLY BUTTERFL
BUTTERFLY BUTTERFLY. BUTTERFLY BUTTERFLY. BUTTERFLY BUTTERFI
BUTTERFLY BUTTERFLY. BUTTERFLY BUTTERFLY. BUTTERFLY BUTTERFI
BUTTERFLY. BUTTERFLY BUTTERFLY. BUTTERFLY BUTTERFLY. BUTTERFI
BUTTERFLY BUTTERFLY. BUTTERFLY BUTTERFLY. BUTTERFLY BUTTERFI
BUTTERFLY. BUTTERFLY BUTTERFLY. BUTTERFLY BUTTERFLY. BUTTERFI
BUTTERFLY. BUTTERFLY BUTTERFLY. BUTTERFLY BUTTERFLY. BUTTERF
BUTTERFLY BUTTERFLY. BUTTERFLY BUTTERFLY. BUTTERFLY BUTTERFI
BUTTERFLY. BUTTERFLY BUTTERFLY. BUTTERFLY BUTTERFLY. BUTTERF
BUTTERFLY BUTTERFLY. BUTTERFLY BUTTERFLY. BUTTERFLY BUTTERF
BUTTERFLY. BUTTERFLY BUTTERFLY. BUTTERFLY BUTTERFLY. BUTTERF
BUTTERFLY BUTTERFLY. BUTTERFLY BUTTERFLY. BUTTERFLY BUTTERF
BUTTERFLY. BUTTERFLY BUTTERFLY. BUTTERFLY BUTTERFLY. BUTTERF
BUTTERFLY BUTTERFLY. BUTTERFLY BUTTERFLY. BUTTERFLY BUTTERF
BUTTERFLY. BUTTERFLY BUTTERFLY. BUTTERFLY BUTTERFLY. BUTTERF
BUTTERFLY BUTTERFLY. BUTTERFLY BUTTERFLY. BUTTERFLY BUTTERF
BUTTERFLY. BUTTERFLY BUTTERFLY. BUTTERFLY BUTTERFLY. BUTTERF
BUTTERFLY BUTTERFLY. BUTTERFLY BUTTERFLY. BUTTERFLY BUTTERE
BUTTERFLY BUTTERFLY. BUTTERFLY BUTTERFLY. BUTTERFLY BUTTERE

Vibrant wings
Flapping into eternity
Enhancing light with inner energy
to break the lovingly
overprotective vines
holding on to save her from herself
But she doesn't need to be saved
She's ready to fly beyond even the vine's
dreams.

acknowledgements

Thanks to the Higher Power for blessing my pen with the power to deliver these words.

Much appreciation extends to my mom Frances, my dad Trevor, my sister Terri and my fiancé Rashad for always reassuring and praising the artist within me. Your love gave me the confidence and support to share parts of myself with strangers.

Special thank you to Marguerite C, Dwight O, and Dara K for taking the time to read this book, and give honest criticism. You made me a better author.

I must also acknowledge the many friends, colleagues and associates who supported, encouraged and inspired me in the creation of this book which includes, but is not limited to Shanice A, Jasmine R, Luther I, Hattresss B, Ameenah A, Tonii L, Jamia J, Shay M, Lianna O, Jenny L, Dieynabou B, Charlene C, Janett C, Celina, Stephan, Nia B, Jennifer, Elmer Q, Shakim H, Harvey L, Kim H, Taneeka W, Brandon L, Imani, Marc C, Alyssa Z, Adrian S, Angela B, Elle T, Jelani G, Ashley A, Melissa R, Jovana W, Tejarshi P, Tiffani, Kamaria, Tilden, Jamise P, Crystal, David P, E Dot M, Tamra, Amanda, Candance, Bong D, Glasiana, Tequila, Maya, Treasure L, Solar C, Sin, Whitney K, Maddie, Anna, Sam, Shauna-Kay N, Open Mic Renegades, Black Greek Poets, and Poetix University.

Through my travels, you have influenced me, and thus my writing. Our experiences together helped these poems take flight in the pages of this book.

And lastly thank you to iiPublishing for helping me bring this dream to life.

the author

nora oz

nora oz is a poetess from Brooklyn, NY who has been writing since the age of 13. She is the co-creator and co-host of InterBoro Mic, a variety show dedicated to highlighting all spoken arts including music, comedy and of course poetry. When nora isn't hosting her own events, she can often be spotted performing at various venues around the city. Her poetry is provocative, mindful, and passionate and is influenced by the transparency of Nikki Giovanni, the storytelling of Stephen King and the passion of Amiri Baraka. She writes on social justice, the condition of the African American woman, family, and whimsical fancies. nora also enjoys whetting palates and stroking imaginations with her erotic poetry. She takes pride in sharing her story and that of her community through spoken word. She encourages the same pride in her students as a member of the Professorial team at Poetix University and part of the administration team of Black Greek Poets. You can follow this dynamic poet on Instagram at @noraoz_queen.

Lightning Source UK Ltd.
Milton Keynes UK
UKHW020659271221
396231UK00008B/265